Beyond the Surface

Exploring the Unconscious Mind with Freud

Freudian Trips

Copyright Page

Disclaimer

The views and opinions expressed in this book are those of the author(s) and do not necessarily reflect the official policy or position of any other agency, organization, employer, or company. The contents of this book are for informational and educational purposes only and are not intended to serve as professional advice, diagnosis, or treatment.

The information provided in this book is believed to be accurate and reliable as of the date of publication. However, it may include some errors or inaccuracies, and no warranty or guarantee is provided regarding the accuracy, timeliness, or applicability of the content.

Readers are encouraged to consult with professional philosophers, educators, or other qualified professionals where appropriate for personalized advice. The author(s) and publisher shall not be liable for any loss, damage, or harm caused or alleged to be caused, directly or indirectly, by the information or ideas contained, suggested, or referenced in this book.

By reading this book, the reader acknowledges and agrees that they are solely responsible for how they interpret and apply the information contained herein.

This book may also include references to other works, studies, and sources. These references are provided for further reading and exploration and do not imply endorsement or validation of the specific theories, viewpoints, or interpretations presented in those works.

Introduction: Meeting Mr. Freud and Your Hidden Mind

Imagine your mind is like a grand old house. There's the front parlor you show visitors, all neatly arranged and well-lit. But then, there's the dusty attic full of forgotten boxes, and even a spooky basement you rarely dare to enter. This is a bit like how Sigmund Freud, a brilliant and rather odd doctor, pictured the human mind.

Freud wasn't the first thinker to wonder what goes on beneath the surface of our thoughts. Yet, he became a revolutionary figure in psychology. He was fascinated by dreams, strange slips of the tongue, and the puzzling ways people would get stuck in unhealthy patterns. Why did we do the things we knew were bad for us? Why did memories we try to forget keep haunting us?

Freud believed most of our mental lives are hidden from ourselves – like that attic and basement. He called this hidden part the "unconscious mind." He proposed that it's a powerful force, bustling with forgotten experiences, secret desires, and uncomfortable feelings we shove out of sight to keep ourselves feeling sane and in control.

This idea was shocking! Imagine telling proper folks in the early 1900s they weren't truly masters of their own minds. Yet, Freud's theories were incredibly influential. Suddenly, people looked differently at dreams, at odd behaviors, even at art and literature. His ideas were imperfect, like any theories, but they opened a new door.

Why Understanding Your Unconscious Matters

Think of a time you blurted out something embarrassing and immediately wished you could take it back. Or perhaps there's a weird fear you have, like of spiders, but you have no idea why. Freud would say these aren't accidents. They're little clues to that hidden part of your mind trying to break through.

Here's where it gets really interesting. Freud believed our unconscious mind plays a much bigger role than we think. It influences why we're attracted to certain people, the choices we make, and even our physical and mental health. Understanding the hidden forces within ourselves can be the first step to untangling our problems and living a life that's more genuinely our own.

Ready to Explore?

Let's get ready for an adventure. There's a fascinating, and sometimes unsettling, world tucked away in our own minds. In the following chapters, we'll peek into your mental attic, descend into the shadowy cellar, and learn what those strange dreams might really mean. Get ready to discover hidden truths about yourself!

Chapter 1: Mapping Your Mental Mansion

Imagine your mind as a huge, multi-level mansion. There are rooms flooded with light, others draped in shadows, and even some locked doors you may not even know exist. This is a bit like how Freud envisioned the way our minds are organized. Let's take a tour and unlock some of those internal doors!

Level 1: The Conscious Mind – The Tip of the Iceberg

This is the part of your mind you're aware of right now. It's where you're reading these words, focusing on understanding, maybe having a side thought about what to eat later. Freud compared it to the tip of an iceberg – just a small fraction of your whole mental world.

Level 2: The Preconscious – The Memory Storage Room

This level is like your mental attic. Things here aren't in your immediate attention, but you can easily bring them up. Your birthday, your phone number, what you did last weekend – it's all tucked away in the preconscious.

Level 3: The Unconscious – The Deep Basement

This is where things get interesting – and messy! Freud believed this is the largest part of our minds. The unconscious is a storage locker for everything we can't comfortably deal with: painful memories, unacceptable urges, hidden anxieties. Most of the time, these stay locked away out of sight.

The Inner Staff: Id, Ego, and Superego

Your mind isn't just rooms; it has a staff always at work! Freud gave these parts funny names:

- **The Id:** This is your inner wild child. It wants what it wants NOW – pleasure, food, comfort – and doesn't care about rules. Think of it like a demanding toddler.
- **The Ego:** The grown-up in the room. It tries to balance the Id's desires with what's realistic and socially acceptable. It's your sense of self, the "I" that makes decisions.
- **The Superego:** Your conscience. This part holds all those shoulds and shouldn't you've picked up from your parents, society, and your own morals. It can be a harsh judge!

When Your Staff Clashes

The Id, Ego, and Superego don't always get along. Imagine that chocolate cake in the fridge. Your Id shouts, "Eat it!" Your Superego says, "You're on a diet!" The Ego is stuck in the middle, trying to figure out a compromise. This inner conflict underlies a lot of our decisions, even if we're not aware of it.

Mind Guards: Defense Mechanisms

When the unconscious mind has things too upsetting to face directly, it has a whole squad of defense mechanisms to keep them hidden. It's like those locked basement doors, and your mind has some clever ways to keep them shut tight:

- **Repression:** Shoving painful stuff down into the unconscious so you don't have to think about it.
- **Denial:** Pretending a problem doesn't exist. ("I'm not really stressed, I'm fine!")
- **Projection:** Blaming others for your own unwanted feelings. ("They're the angry one, not me!")

Why It Matters

This might seem like silly mind games, but it's incredibly important. Our minds work hard to maintain a certain image of ourselves. When the hidden parts try to poke through, it causes a lot of internal chaos. Understanding how your mind is structured, and how it protects itself, can help you start unraveling why you think, feel, and act the way you do.

Let's Keep Exploring!

This was just a quick tour of your mental mansion. There's a lot more to discover in the chapters ahead: mysterious dreams, strange slip-ups, and why, sometimes, we self-sabotage even when we want the best for ourselves. Ready to keep peeking behind those internal doors?

Chapter 2: Decoding Your Nighttime Movies

Have you ever woken up from a dream that was so vivid, so bizarre, or maybe even downright disturbing, that it stuck with you all day? Freud believed that dreams are like windows into the hidden world of our unconscious mind. They may seem nonsensical, but he saw them as coded messages.

The Dream Double Feature: Manifest vs. Latent

Freud thought every dream has two layers:

- **Manifest Content:** This is the surface story, the actual images, and events you remember. Think of it as the movie you watched during sleep – a girl flying, a monster chase, losing all your teeth.
- **Latent Content:** This is the hidden meaning, the symbolic representation of your unconscious desires, fears, and conflicts. It's like the director's commentary to the dream movie, revealing what it's *really* all about.

Your Wish Is the Dream's Command

Freud had a rather provocative idea: he believed all dreams, even scary ones, are a form of wish fulfillment. Now, this doesn't mean you *want* to be chased by a zombie. It means that deep down, there's something else your mind wants to express, and it disguises it within the dream's weird story.

Imagine dreaming about failing an exam you're nervous about. On the surface, it's anxiety. But perhaps there's a hidden wish to escape the pressure, or even an unconscious fear of success. Decoding the dream can give you clues about the tangled feelings beneath the surface.

Dream Language 101: It's All About Symbols

Our unconscious mind doesn't speak in plain English. It loves symbols! That's why dreams often seem so random. Freud believed some symbols are fairly universal, while others are personal to the dreamer. Here are some common examples:

- **Falling:** Feeling out of control, insecure, or overwhelmed.
- **Flying:** Freedom, ambition, or escaping a difficult situation.
- **Naked in Public:** Vulnerability, fear of being exposed or judged.
- **Houses:** Often symbolize the self. Different rooms may represent different aspects of personality.

Dream Detective: Finding Meaning

It's important to remember there's no one-size-fits-all dream dictionary. The key is to look at your dream, then pay attention to the emotions you felt and your own life experiences. Ask yourself:

- What stands out as the most striking or odd thing in the dream?
- How did it make me feel when I dreamt it, and how do I feel about it now?
- Does anything in the dream connect to things going on in my waking life?

The Fun and the Challenge of Dream Interpretation

Analyzing dreams can be intriguing, sometimes even a bit addictive! It's like solving a puzzle. But it can also be frustrating. Don't get discouraged if a dream remains stubbornly mysterious. Sometimes, just being curious about them opens the door to your unconscious a little wider.

Let Your Dreams Speak

Dreams are your mind's own personal art form – weird, sometimes wonderful, and always revealing something about your inner world. Pay attention to them, write them down, mull them over. With a little practice, you might be surprised by the messages you start to decode from those strange nighttime movies!

Chapter 3: The Unconscious Strikes Again! Catching Your Mind Off-Guard

Remember Freud's idea that the unconscious is like a hidden room in your mental mansion? Well, even with the best security, sometimes things slip out. Here's where it gets fun – we're going to look at those everyday moments when our unconscious mind accidentally takes the spotlight.

Oops! Did I Just Say That? – The Truth in Slips

Ever called your current partner by your ex's name? Or referred to your coworker as "Mom"? Major cringe! Freud had a name for these verbal hiccups: "Freudian Slips". He believed they weren't just random mistakes, but clues bubbling up from our unconscious.

Think of your mind like a pot on the stove. Even if you try to keep a lid on things like secret resentments, attraction to someone you shouldn't like, or anxieties you don't want to face, those feelings simmer below. Sometimes, the pressure gets too high and *whoosh!* your true thoughts escape via slip of the tongue.

Laughing Matters: Jokes and Your Inner Conflicts

Why do we laugh at things that are a little wrong, or that touch on taboo topics? Freud thought humor was a clever release valve for our unconscious. Jokes often play with our anxieties about things like sex, aggression, or social rules.

Imagine all those jokes about nagging mothers-in-law. On the surface, they're funny. But they tap into a common human struggle - tensions within families, feeling judged, desiring control. Humor allows us to release a tiny bit of that tension in a safe, socially acceptable way.

When the Unconscious Gets Stuck: Neurosis

Freud was a doctor dealing with patients that had real mental suffering – anxiety that wouldn't ease, phobias that wrecked lives, or repeating unhealthy patterns. He labeled this "neurosis" and believed it stemmed from old, unresolved conflicts in the unconscious mind.

Imagine your mental basement is packed with boxes of uncomfortable emotions you haven't dealt with. Instead of opening them, you just keep piling more stuff on top. Eventually, the whole structure gets shaky. That's a bit like how those unconscious conflicts can erupt as mental health issues.

Psychoanalysis: Shining a Light in the Basement

Freud's revolutionary idea was to treat these issues not by focusing just on symptoms, but by exploring what's hidden deep within the mind. This is where psychoanalysis came in. Think of it as guided exploration of the mental house with a therapist.

Techniques like talking freely about anything that comes to mind (free association) and analyzing dreams, were seen as ways to uncover unconscious patterns. The goal wasn't a quick fix, but a gradual understanding of yourself that could lead to lasting change and relief.

The Unconscious Is Everywhere

From accidental word swaps to the jokes that make you giggle nervously, the unconscious is always at play. It impacts how you relate to others, the choices you make, and even your well-being.

Understanding these hidden forces isn't about diagnosing yourself with deep, dark problems. It's a way to get a little more curious and compassionate about the strange, wonderful, and messy ways your mind works. You might be surprised what you discover!

Chapter 4: Growing Up Messy: Freud's Stages of Development

Get ready for a whirlwind tour of childhood – with a Freudian twist! Freud believed that our experiences during those early years have a HUGE impact on our adult personality. It wasn't all about diapers and potty training; he saw these stages as simmering pots of conflicts, desires, and developing identities.

The Roadmap of Development (Freud-Style)

Freud proposed five stages of psychosexual development. The "sexual" part isn't just about grown-up stuff; it's more about pleasure and how our bodies and minds mature. Here's the breakdown:

1. **Oral Stage (Birth to About 1 Year):** Baby world revolves around the mouth – sucking, eating, exploring. If needs here aren't met well, Freud thought it could lead to adult issues like dependency, pessimism, or habits like nail-biting.

2. **Anal Stage (1-3 Years):** Potty training central! It's a battle of control between the child gaining independence and the parents setting limits. Being too harsh or too lax here could lead to fixations like being overly concerned with orderliness, or the opposite – being rebellious and chaotic.

3. **Phallic Stage (3-6 Years):** Kids become aware of bodies and gender differences. This is where Freud hit controversy with the Oedipus Complex (boys desiring moms, seeing dads as rivals) and Electra Complex (girls the reverse). He believed working through these is key to healthy identity.

4. **Latency Stage (6-Puberty):** A calmer time. Sexual urges quiet down, kids focus on school, friends. Here, Freud thought problems didn't necessarily start, but unresolved stuff from earlier stages could simmer under the surface.

5. **Genital Stage (Puberty Onward):** Hormones surge, adult sexuality awakens. If all went well earlier, folks form healthy relationships. If not, old fixations may cause trouble in love and intimacy.

Fixations: When the Growing Gets Stuck

Imagine each stage is a level in a video game. If you don't pass the challenges, you can get stuck. Freud used the word "fixation". Like being obsessed with order because you didn't have enough control as a toddler, or being clingy in relationships if early needs for comfort weren't met.

The Oedipus/Electra Debate: Uncomfortable Truths?

Freud's most disputed ideas! Critics find them outdated and focused too much on sexuality. But think about it this way: those complexes are really about how tiny kids, in their limited understanding, grapple with love, rivalry, and figuring out their place in the family. This has lifelong echoes!

Is Freud the Final Word?

Absolutely not! His stages were very specific, and lots of folks develop just fine even if they had slightly bumpy childhoods. But Freud opened a HUGE debate about the importance of early experiences. Here's the takeaway:

- Childhood matters: How we are nurtured and treated shapes us in profound ways.
- We carry our past: Even stuff we don't remember may linger, influencing how we act without realizing it.
- Change is possible: Understanding these patterns is the first step towards choosing differently and creating a healthier life.

Growing up is complicated. Freud made it even messier, but also a whole lot more fascinating. Understanding his ideas helps us understand ourselves, and those we love, on a deeper level.

Chapter 5: The Man Who Shook the World – Freud's Shadow and its Critics

Freud wasn't just a doctor with a couch and some wacky ideas. He was like an earthquake that cracked open how we see the human mind. His influence wasn't always pretty, but it was undeniably huge! Let's look at the aftershocks and the critics who questioned if he was all he was cracked up to be.

Freud's Fingerprint: Everywhere You Look

- **Therapy Revamped:** Before Freud, mental illness was misunderstood or dismissed. He insisted on seeking root causes in the mind, not just the body. Though psychoanalysis looks different today, this focus on the inner world is HUGE.
- **Art Explosion:** Artists loved Freud's focus on dreams, symbols, the irrational! It inspired movements like Surrealism, with its melting clocks and bizarre landscapes. Think of it unlocking the imagination.
- **Unmasking Literature:** Suddenly characters weren't just good or bad. Critics dissected them with Freudian

theories, seeing hidden drives, Oedipal desires...
books weren't innocent anymore!

- **Everyday Speak:** Ever heard someone called "anal
retentive" or joked about having an Oedipus complex?
Freud's terms invaded our language, even if we use
them loosely.

Cracks in the Theory: The Doubters Speak Up

Freud was brilliant, but not perfect. Here's where his critics
pounced:

- **Too Much Sex?** While Freud opened the door to
talking about sexuality's impact, he might have gone
overboard reducing EVERYTHING to childhood sexual
conflicts.
- **Science or Stories?** Freud based ideas on his
patients, mostly well-off Victorian ladies. That's hardly
a sample of all humanity! His theories lacked the
rigorous testing modern science demands.
- **Male Gaze:** Freud was obsessed with male
experience, often neglecting women's psychology.
Feminist thinkers definitely had plenty to challenge
there!

The Neo-Freudians: Agreeing to Disagree

Some of Freud's own students became his biggest
challengers! They took his core ideas, but spun them in new
ways:

- **Carl Jung:** Less sex, more spirituality. He focused on the "collective unconscious", ancient myths and symbols he thought we all share.
- **Alfred Adler:** Stressed social forces, not just inner ones. He talked of the "inferiority complex" and how striving for power shapes us.
- **Karen Horney:** Finally, a female voice! She fought Freud's sexism, and emphasized cultural and relationship influences on our psychology.

Was Freud Right?

The answer is a mixed bag. Parts of his theory definitely don't hold up today. Yet, here's why he still matters:

- **The Talking Cure:** Though his methods evolved, Freud championed the idea that talking about our inner world, even the messy stuff, can be healing.
- **Power of the Unconscious:** Even if he exaggerated it, he made us acknowledge that there's far more than meets the eye to our motivations and actions.
- **Permission to be Human:** In an era that demanded rigid rules, Freud told us it's okay to be irrational, conflicted, a bit weird. That was actually liberating!

Freud may be a slightly tarnished legend now. He was both a product of his time, and far ahead of it. His work is a fascinating, sometimes flawed, landmark that forever changed how we explore what it means to be human.

Chapter 6: The Unconscious Gets an Upgrade – Your Mind in the 21st Century

Freud would probably either be fascinated or horrified by the world today! His old couch and notebooks have been replaced with brain scanners and sophisticated therapies. Yet, even in the age of technology, those hidden forces of the unconscious are still at play. Let's dive in!

Brain vs. Mind: Neuroscience Weighs In

Remember that mental mansion Freud imagined? Well, neuroscience gives us blueprints! Brain imaging lets us peek at what's firing up when we feel, think, or even dream. Here's the fascinating debate:

- Support for Freud: Scans show that emotional centers of the brain are super active even when we're not consciously aware of what's bothering us. Freud was onto something about those hidden emotions!
- Challenges: The brain is complex. The neat split into Id, Ego, Superego doesn't map onto precise brain

regions. The unconscious may be less structured than Freud thought.
- New Mysteries: Brain science raises its own questions – do we truly have free will if so much occurs on an unconscious level?

Therapy Evolved: Unlocking the Unconscious (Without a 10-Year Analysis)

Talking about your feelings is still powerful, but modern therapy has gotten more targeted when it comes to the unconscious:

- Focusing on the Body: Trauma-informed therapies understand that we hold experiences not just in our minds, but in our bodies. They include movement, breathwork, etc. to release what's stuck.
- Targeting Patterns: Therapies like CBT help you identify unconscious thought patterns driving anxiety or bad habits. Then, you learn to replace them – reprogramming your mind!
- The Unconscious in the Moment: Some therapists focus on what comes up in the room between patient and therapist, as a clue to unconscious relationship patterns at play in the client's life.

The Hidden Persuaders: Your Unconscious Goes Shopping

Ever buy something, then wonder "Why did I need this?" Freud would chuckle knowingly. Advertisers and corporations are masters at tapping into our unconscious!

- Pretty Colors, Primitive Brain: Packaging in soothing or exciting colors taps into deep emotional responses, bypassing rational decision-making.
- The Need to Belong: Ads selling a lifestyle, not just a product, play on anxieties about not fitting in. If everyone cool has those jeans… your unconscious does the math!
- Instant Pleasure: Online shopping, with its one-click ease, is like the Id triumphant…want it, get it, NOW! Downsides (like the credit card bill) come later.

Can We Outsmart Our Unconscious?

A little bit! While it'll always be a powerful force, greater self-awareness helps. Here's how:

- Name That Feeling: Before reacting, take a breath. Is it true anger, or an old hurt flaring up? Identifying the emotion gives you back some control.
- Pause Before Purchase: Is it a need or a craving? Delaying instant gratification lets your rational mind catch up to your desire.
- Know Your Triggers: What sets off your temper, or makes you fall into unhealthy patterns? Awareness is the first step towards choosing a different response.

The Journey Continues…

Freud opened a door that we're still walking through. The unconscious mind will always be slightly shadowy, and that's okay. Modern science and therapy give us new tools, but the same goal remains: to understand the hidden forces that shape us, and use that knowledge to live more freely and authentically.

Conclusion: Beyond the Surface – Your Journey of Self-Discovery

We've journeyed together through a strange and fascinating landscape – the world of Freud's ideas. Along the way, we've unlocked musty mental attics, decoded bizarre dreams, and battled inner demons named Id and Superego. It's been quite a ride!

So, was Freud a genius, a madman, or something in between? The truth is, he was a pioneer. He dared to dive into the murky depths of the human mind at a time when most people preferred to keep things neatly on the surface. His theories may not all withstand scrutiny, but he started a conversation we're still having today.

Here's why Freud's legacy matters:

- **No More Shame:** He made it okay to admit we're not always rational, in control, or understand our own motivations. That was a surprisingly radical act for his time!

- **The Power of Story:** Freud showed how our personal stories, from childhood onwards, shape who we become. This understanding is vital for healing and change.
- **The Unconscious Endures:** While the details have evolved, the idea that hidden forces influence us is supported by both modern science and everyday experience.

This isn't just about history or old theories. This book has been an invitation to turn the lens of curiosity onto yourself. Here's how to keep the exploration going:

- **Dream Detective:** Keep a dream journal. Even if you don't understand them fully, tuning into those nighttime stories can be surprisingly insightful.
- **Notice the Slip-Ups:** Did you make an odd verbal blunder? Instead of cringing, ask yourself playfully, "What was my mind trying to say there?"
- **Question Your Autopilot:** We all have habits and reactions that are hard to shake. Next time you find yourself in one, pause and ask, "Where does this come from? Does it still serve me?"

Understanding your unconscious mind isn't about achieving perfection, or becoming some kind of walking psychology textbook. It's about self-compassion, a sense of humor about our shared human messiness, and the freedom that comes from knowing there's always more to discover.

Freud may have been a controversial figure, but he left us with an enduring gift: a sense of wonder about the hidden depths within us all. The journey of exploring your own unconscious is one that lasts a lifetime. Are you ready to take the next step?

About Freudian Trips

Welcome to Freudian Trips, your dedicated platform for diving deep into the world of psychology. We are more than just a YouTube channel or a book publisher. We are a beacon of enlightenment, making complex psychological concepts accessible and engaging for all.

Our YouTube channel is a rich repository of psychology made simple. We take the profound and often complex ideas from the world of psychology and break them down into digestible, easy-to-understand content. From the foundational theories of Freud to the cognitive insights of Piaget, we cover a broad spectrum of psychological schools and thoughts, making psychology accessible to everyone, regardless of their background or prior knowledge.

As a book publisher, we take the same approach, transforming intricate psychological theories into comprehensible narratives. Our books are not just collections of words, but vessels of wisdom that make psychology approachable and relatable. We believe that psychology should not be confined to academic circles, but should be available to all who seek to understand the human mind and behavior.

At Freudian Trips, we believe in the power of curiosity and the pursuit of knowledge. We are here to stoke the fires of your curiosity, to guide you on your intellectual journey, and to help you navigate the fascinating world of psychology.

If you are someone who is not afraid to question, to explore, and to learn, then you are in the right place. Join us on this journey of exploration, as we make psychology easy to understand, one concept at a time.

Be sure to visit our Youtube channel at:
www.freudiantrips.com/youtube

You can also visit us on the web at www.freudiantrips.com

Welcome to The Freudian Trip community. Stay curious. Stay enlightened.